# THE

# FIGHT

# OF MY

# LIFE

**Natai Billops**

Copyright © 2018 Natai Billops

Scripture quotations are from the King James Version of the Holy Bible unless otherwise indicated.

ISBN: 978-0-692-17553-8

Cover Design by: Her Book Bar

Edited by:

Spirit of Excellence Writing & Editing Services, LLC
www.TakeUpThySword.com

# **<u>Dedication</u>**

*The Fight of My Life*, is dedicated to all those who are in the midst of the most trying time of their lives. You have reached the point where you do not know whether to stay or to go. You are not sure if you should go left or right. In spite of what you see now, know that you have an expected end. Your expected end is that you win. Regardless of the present, things must turn around in your favor because you were destined to win each and every battle that you face.

# Table of Contents

# __Down and Out__

*Come unto me, all ye that labour and are heavy laden,
and I will give you rest.*
*Matthew 11:28*

If you've ever gone through something at all in life, then you at one time or another felt down and out. Contrary to what we may feel and what we may believe, down and out is not a place at all. It is, however, a mentality that we develop when tribulations occur in our lives. If we could see the bigger picture, we would notice that the concept of being down and out is merely where we trap our thoughts when things are not moving in ways that we would like. Proverbs 23:7 tells us that as a man thinks in his heart, so is he. Here we have proof that if we think we are down and out, we'll believe it; and if we believe it, we'll surely act as if we are.

Most times when we are going through, we focus solely on what we are dealing with and how we feel; we give life to the problem instead of looking for the one thing that may make the turmoil we are facing worthwhile. As a result of our focus being in the wrong place, we neglect the opportunity to learn through what we are experiencing. What are your thoughts saying about what you're experiencing? Are your thoughts causing you to believe that your current place is your final destination? Or are they bringing to the surface a much better perspective than what reality presents to you?

When we shift our thinking, we begin to look for other ways to view our situations. Shifting our thinking forces us to take a new approach. It causes us to see things in a different light. Shifting our thinking puts us in a position where we no longer see things as they are but rather, we look to what they can be. When we shift our thinking in the right direction, we bring hope to a hopeless situation and mentally become conquerors before the battle is won.

An alternative to feeling sorry for yourself would be to find out how you arrived to the place where you currently are. Before we go further, understand that sometimes you end up in certain places not because of anything you've done, but because of where God is taking you. Some tribulations are inevitable and are necessary for your growth. However on the other hand, we can sometimes make choices—whether knowingly or unknowingly—that lead us down a path that we never intended to take. As a result, we must deal with the penalties that have been set aside for the choices we have made.

While it may be true that sometimes we put ourselves in situations that don't always go as we would have planned, even those situations will play a role in shaping and developing us into who we need to be in order to reach the next level in life. So it's not really a loss but more of what some like to call a blessing in disguise. Just when it looked as if things couldn't go even more left, something happens and things violently shift; and right before your eyes, you see things coming together in a way that would not have happened unless they first fell apart.

If you find after searching that maybe you made a wrong turn along the way that brought you to where you currently are, seek direction so that you can get on the right track. If you are someone who has made a wrong turn, here is what you may notice, returning to the right path may not be a simple task. Wrong turns usually equate to detours. Just because you've noticed that you've made a mistake does not necessarily mean that everything will turn around and return to normal. You could possibly be required to finish your detour before returning to the regularly scheduled program. Acknowledging the mistake once it has already been made only ensures that you've taken heed to what has gone wrong. It doesn't even guarantee that you won't revert to the same behavior in the future. This, again, requires a well thought out choice to be made.

This is why it is important that we think about the consequences to our actions. When events take place, we must remember that subevents will stem from them. The nature of those subevents depends directly upon the action we chose to participate in or commit. We can't always be so focused on the now; we must take later into consideration. How does your attitude influence tomorrow? Is your way of thinking conducive to a successful future? Are we making sound decisions that will have a positive impact on our future? Are we thinking about the latter as we are simultaneously making choices for the present?

Here is where maturity is important. Although things may sound good, that does not necessarily mean that we need to involve ourselves in them. It is important that we learn to have discernment about the actions we take. Every place we visit or every person we decide to hang out with may not be connected to our destiny. When we busy ourselves with people, places, and things that hold no future in our lives, we move further away from our destiny. I wish I could say that the further you get from your destiny, the harder things may seem, but I can't. The reality is that the closer you get to your destiny, you may find that things are just as hectic. However, I pose this question to you: Would you rather face trouble closer to or further from your purposed destination? With destiny comes protection and security. So regardless of how things may seem, if we are closer to our destined place, our trials will be more manageable.

We must discuss unfavorable options. And by this I mean those opportunities that present themselves to us, but we reject them because they're not what we we're looking for. So many times, we paralyze ourselves because we overlook what is for us because it doesn't come in a way that we expected. We unconsciously choose to remain where we are because we refuse to accept what God allows. We refuse to accept the blessing God has handmade just for us. But God is challenging us to take on the uncomfortable thing because the uncomfortable thing will somehow bring us the most needed comfortability—the level of comfortability that will grace us for what is to come.

Unfortunately, there comes times when we begin to settle into what we are in. We become content with the mentality of being down and out and adopt it as a norm. The truth is, we become content in such a low mentality when we forget who we are and who we were created to be. Let's make this clear: don't become so content in your struggle that you allow it to become a norm for you. It's not where you are supposed to stay but rather, a pit stop as you move forward into greater things.

We must also be careful not to reject what was intended to work for our good. It is easy to run away when we know that running will take us away from the things that seem to be hurting us the most, but running is not always the best choice. It is necessary that we stand our ground because what may seem to be hurting us could very well be building us up.

The thing about being down and out is that if you are not careful, you will not recognize where you are until it is too late. This mentality begins with what you would simply call a bad day. However, that bad day somehow turns into a routine and you allow it to become your reality. And to think, it all starts because we cannot see the light from the dark places that we encounter in life.

This is why we must be cautious and aware of our feelings and emotions. We give our feelings and emotions so much power and allow them to dictate our outcomes. We allow feelings and emotions to interfere and prohibit progression all because we would rather cater to them than to speak to them and command that they be subject to where we are going and not where we are. If we aren't careful, our feelings and emotions can lead us to believe that we are down and out when in reality, all we need to do is come up for air.

We must be sure to catch ourselves before we fall. If we can identify that we operate with a down and out mentality, we can watch for things that support that mentality and cause us to sink deeper. This provokes an evaluation. That evaluation must include a self-evaluation. We must take a look at our surroundings, including those people we choose to associate with and the places we choose to go. It is important that we examine our lives at the time this mentality has tried to hit. What has been going on that could further encourage and entertain this mentality that you must rid yourself of?

You can only remain down and out if you allow yourself to be held captive of those things which attempt to hold you down. The thing about being down and out is that it forces you to have an expected end. We have discussed that the concept of being down and out is merely a mentality that we adapt based on our position. Again, let's look at this from a new perspective: If your current position is low, then you have absolutely no choice but to aim high. In the words of Michele Obama, "When they go low, we go high." When the enemy aims low and knocks you down, you must aim high in order to defeat him.

So while you are down and out, and begin to experience your low place (because it's inevitable and a part of the process), you must think on those things that are true, honest, just, pure, lovely, and of good report (Philippians 4:8). You should think of the best and not the worst. We can sometimes allow ourselves to become so consumed with what we are in that we forget that brighter days are an option for us. Because the only place to go is up, your status will soon change. So if you are broke, you will soon be rich. If you are sick, you will soon be healthy. If you are depressed, you will soon experience happiness. When we begin to look at where we are going and spend less time focusing on where we are, things begin to shift in our favor.

Be intentional about setting yourself up for elevation. Elevation is simply moving higher than where you currently are. We must be careful not to become what we are going through. Participate in activities that will help you climb the ladder and reach a higher point, and be someone greater than who you are now. So ask yourself: What can I learn while I'm down and out?

What is God trying to teach me? What is he trying to tell me? What is he trying to do in and through me?

Sometimes we get so caught up in our low place and how we feel in our position that we forget that God is still moving even at the most difficult times. God is still working even in your low place. He is still able to minister a word to you, but you have to open up your heart and your ears and be in a place where you can receive exactly what it is that God is trying to say to you in that moment.

We must change our perspective and how we are looking at where we are. Once we change our mindset, then we position ourselves to think up, to think bigger, and to think better. It's only then that we can become who we are supposed to be. All the things that we encounter and that we face were not meant to break us but only to build us. It is not until you change your perspective that you can grab ahold of that concept.

Now sometimes it is hard to get to a place where we can acknowledge where we are and be okay with it enough to do something about it. However, in order to set ourselves up to excel, exceed, and elevate, we must acknowledge where we are. But that does not mean we have to accept where we are; acknowledge it and strive for more. This is when you must ask yourself: Am I really content with where I am? If your answer is yes, then you will simply remain where you are because you have become comfortable in a place that should have only been used to push you into a new dimension. As a result, you won't strive for more.

On the other hand, if your answer is no, you would do all that it takes to get out of the pit that you are in. If your answer is no, you understand that being down and being out is not a final destination but rather, a place that is taking you to where you were destined to be in the first place. Sometimes it gets hard; however, if we are not content and do not settle where we are, we can strive, we can be better, we can go higher, we can achieve, and we can live on purpose.

You will not always have people with you at your lowest point. Sometimes your lowest point consists of just you and God. God instructs us to come to him when we were weary or burdened and he would give us rest; for his yoke is easy and his burden is light (Matthew 11:28,30 NIV). What are you doing when it is just you and God? How are you reacting to the trials and tribulations? How are you battling the strongholds that you sometimes have to carry? You have to remember that God is with you and he is pulling you through and helping you to be the best you that you can be.

While experiencing your down and out moment, be careful not to look to others for empathy or sympathy. There is a chance that many will not understand what you are going through. When you expose your turmoil to those who do not understand, you risk receiving discouragement instead of encouragement. When people do not understand but still offer advice, they bring defeat instead of helping you on your way to victory. This is a crucial time for you, and who you allow to whisper in your ear has a direct impact on how you progress. We may wish to share our dark place with others in an attempt to get words of wisdom to keep us afloat but sometimes, it's best to go through alone. You are the only person who will receive the good or the bad in the end, and sometimes it is just necessary to quiet all the noise. Too many opinions can lead to distractions. So sometimes the best thing said is nothing at all.

Separation may be just what you need to get you through. Think it not strange that at your lowest point, you may have to disconnect from people who you were once close to. It may be painful but separation and disconnection are sometimes the necessary ingredients for growth. Consider growing pains: they may not feel good, but the end result makes the pain worth it. You cannot avoid the growing pains. God will never force you to do anything, but sometimes he will put you in an uncomfortable position that forces you to move.

Truth be told, we are usually reluctant to what God would have us to do because we look at where we are and we cannot comprehend what God wants to do in our lives. We create an atmosphere of stagnation around us that ultimately feeds the mentality that we already have of being down and out. We will only remain down and out for as long as we allow ourselves. The enemy glories in our low place but once we decide to take back the sound mind that God has given us, we will begin to notice a change not only in our thinking, but in our lives.

Are you willing to come out of hiding and confront your battle head on? You can't win if you choose to remain behind the scenes.

What would have happened if David had never shown up to fight Goliath? The giant would not have been defeated; but more importantly, David would have never recognized his own strength. Just like David, we have been called to slay the giants that may arise in our lives; but in order to make a difference, we have to show up. We must have the courage to show up to the fight in spite of the condition that we are in.

# **Key Points**

# **Key Points**

# I've Fallen, but I Can Get Up

*For a just man falleth seven times, and riseth up again:*
*but the wicked shall fall into mischief.*

*Proverbs 24:16*

"Help, I've fallen and I can't get up!" I can't help but to think about the Life Alert commercial where it shows an elderly person falling and thereafter, calling out for help. These commercials usually consist of the elderly person being alone in a position where they cannot help themselves. They know that in order to get up, they will need help. Most times, they are wearing a necklace that has an emergency call button. In the time of need, they can push the button and help will be on the way.

Just like those people in the Life Alert commercials, some of us have encountered things in life and we feel that once we fall, we need help in order to get up. However, what if I told you that although you have fallen, although you may have slipped up, although you may have done the wrong thing, you still have the ability to get up? Because when God is within you, you cannot fail.

21

Understand that a lot happens mentally, emotionally, and spiritually when someone falls. Sometimes we take advantage of our trials and tribulations and subconsciously become the host of a pity party, inviting all of our loved ones to attend. We allow ourselves to become subject to what we have gone through. The reality is that although you may have fallen, you have to tap into the resources you have access to so you can get back up. You may have fallen hard but despite the hurt, you still have life; so that means that you can still get up.

We have to understand that when we fall, we are properly positioned to seek God's face and to hear God's voice. How do you get up after being so low, you might ask. Well, you must take advantage of how you are positioned and begin to pray and hear all that God is trying to say to you. The truth is, being down is the only way that you can get up. Instead of viewing your fall as a bad thing, look from the perspective that you are in the perfect position to pray your way up. You have obtained the perfect posture to reach God and hear from Heaven. So while you are down, reposition yourself so that you may rest on your knees and have an encounter with God.

While you are down and while you have fallen subject to this low place, God is still speaking and giving instruction. It is up to you to listen closely.

There are three types of people: the ones who pray all of the time, the ones who only pray when things are good, and those who only pray when things are bad. I have struggled with praying in the bad times. It always seemed that when things went left, my prayers left with them. While we should strive to have a consistent prayer life, prayer in the bad times is so important because it gives us the fight we need to overcome whatever we are enduring. If we fail to speak to God or open our ears so that we can hear from him, we let the enemy in; and when he arrives, he brings his army, and they are prepared to tear us down.

Wouldn't it be great if we took our pitfalls as an opportunity to get to know God on a deeper level? The truth is, God would not put us in predicaments that we could not get out of. He strategically aligned every hardship with our purpose. They are designed so that we can win and be victorious in the end. If what you face is

23

purposed pointed, then know that no matter what, you can come out on top.

Although we may fall, we must realize that falling does not mean that it is the end. We must stop equating tough times with death. There is a well-known saying that goes, "What doesn't kill you only makes you stronger." And when we grab ahold of the concept that is presented through that saying, we realize that situations may come our way, but that does not mean that we cannot win in the end. So even if you currently find yourself on the ground, understand that as long as you are breathing, you still possess the necessary fight within you to get back up. Although you may be hurt, you still have a life full of destiny and purpose that you must fulfill. If you are still living, that means you still have the strength to push through it and get up.

If you wish to be something great, the ideal thing to do would be to surround yourself with winners. Surround yourself with people you aspire to be like. When you do, you expose yourself to the greatness that you wish to obtain. There is something about being in the company of people who are at the place you are trying to reach.

They can coach you, they can teach you, they can correct you, and they can help you excel to your next level. So if you find yourself in a fallen state, look for those who can help you get up. There will always be some who stick around so that they can specifically see our downfall, and that is okay. We must understand that everyone who is around us does not want to see our come up.

First Corinthians 15:33 instructs us not to be deceived because evil communications corrupt good manners. For this reason, we must be careful of whom we allow in our inner circle. If those you associate yourself with do not speak words of affirmation and encouragement to you, it is necessary to reconsider their presence in your life. If the people you choose to have around you cannot recognize when you are off of your square and cannot be committed to helping you get up when you fall, it is time to ponder on whether or not they have your best interests at heart.

These are the people we must look out for. They appear to be our friends but in reality, they wish that we remain where we are. These are the people who like to see us do good as long as we do not do better than them. These are the people who advise us as long as their advice can keep us at the same level or lower than them. It is important that you use discernment when it comes to the people you surround yourself with. Everyone who appears to be a friend is not a friend.

Just think about it: Judas appeared to be in covenant with Jesus but as we all know, he betrayed him as if he never knew him at all. We can even think of how Peter denied Jesus. These were two of the closest people to Jesus but when times got hard and when things became difficult, Judas and Peter turned their backs on Jesus. They became uncomfortable and could not stand their ground. Just like them, sometimes people can only support you until they become uncomfortable; it is at this time that their true colors are exposed.

Wrong company will always keep you bound while proclaiming to be on your side. Imagine if Judas and Peter had not betrayed and denied Jesus: Would Jesus had ever made it to the cross? Would Jesus had ever saved humanity? Would our sins be forgiven? Would we have access to the Father through the Son? I pose these questions to help you to understand that even lost relationships are a part of God's plan. If some people stay, then the plan of God may not prevail; and our ultimate goal should be to live the life that God has purposed for us.

Being in covenant with God gives us the keys to survive. When we are in relationship with God and know who he is, we make ourselves available to strategies that the ordinary person may not have access to. What may be difficult for one person may be something that we can easily deal with simply because we are connected to and in relationship with the one who has orchestrated where we are. God gives us the grace to endure whatever it is that we face. And because we have the grace to go through, that same grace will bring us out and equip us for the next time we are challenged in our walk.

Understanding is also important if we wish to survive. Although we may not always understand where we are or where we are going, we understand that all things work together for our good (Romans 8:28). While what we may be experiencing may not necessarily be comfortable, the uncomfortable places in which we find ourselves are just what we need to groom us for the next place that God has for us.

When you have fallen, this is not the time to throw away your keys of relationship with God and understanding. You have to hold tight to these keys and put them to use. What good are they if you allow them to sit and lie dormant at the most opportune time? These keys have a purpose, but it is up to you to activate the purpose that lies within these tools.

I challenge you to make the best out of your low place. This is not a time to be embarrassed but rather, it's a time when you can discover a new you. While you are down, do your best to not look like what you are going through. If the wrong people can sense that you are in the middle of a tough time, they will try to use that to their advantage and make light of your troubled time. Everything isn't for everyone to know and exposing your hardships to the wrong people could end up pulling you lower than where you already are. By any means, protect your fallen place. After all, your fallen place is a part of your destiny, and every aspect of your destiny should be protected. Do not allow just anyone to offer assistance.

All assistance is not good assistance, and the wrong assistance could lead you in the wrong direction.

What if when we fell we did not contemplate getting up, rather we just did it? Contemplation leaves room for doubt. We become so much more powerful when we realize that falling does not have to be the end factor. Even if life hurts us on the way down, being determined to get back up—regardless of what we face—can make a difference not only in the outcome, but in who we become.

Think of a baby learning to walk: Although they fall, they get back up because that is the only way to progress and master the craft of walking. If they remain down then they will never understand the concept of learning something that is a necessity to make it through life. You cannot move forward if you choose to stay bound. Now that baby learning to walk may have people around them cheering them on, but we must learn to be our own cheerleader if times call for it. We must be sure not to depend on people to cheer us on. If no one is watching, can you still perform a specific task? If no one is around, can you still rise above the fall? The ones we expect to support us are sometimes the ones we cannot seem to find when we feel as though we need them the most. This should never dictate our next move.

While being down, it may be necessary to get delivered from people and their opinions. And once we reach this level of deliverance, it won't matter who is around. We must remain committed to getting up and pressing forward because there is still work to be done. If we fall and choose to remain down, that does not eliminate the trial; it actually adds to it. We then begin to prolong the storm. Giving up then turns into more than what we bargained for.

To fall may be a position, but it does not have to be your final condition. Determine in your mind to get back up regardless of whatever knocked you down. You do not have to be committed to a place that prevents you from reaching your destiny. We always assume that our fallen place is a thing, but we must broaden our imagination and realize that our fallen state could be a variety of things. It could be a decision that you made or it could be people you have encountered. You may not have the power to undo what has already taken place, but you do have the power to move past where you are. If you find that you have fallen, this is how you can get up:

First, acknowledge the fall. The only thing worse than not acknowledging the fall is pretending that it never happened. There is more to acknowledging a fall than just simply stating that you have fallen. To acknowledge means to examine and discover how you fell in the first place. Falling may sometimes require repentance. If we were to be honest, sometimes we do things that are no good for us and falling is only the consequence of our action. Even with this being the case, you do not have to remain where you are. The act of true repentance should cause a change of heart and ensure that you do not repeat actions that bring you to the same predicament in the future. So acknowledging how and why you have reached this place can position you so that you never have to visit it again. Acknowledgement is important because it shows that you understand where you are. It is easy for us to conclude that we do not wish to return back to a place once we realize the impact it has had on us.

After acknowledging the fall, you must make up in your mind that you want to move beyond where you are. If you have no desire to get up, the chances of you getting up are slim to none. You must find the motivation inside of you that will push you even when you don't feel like moving. Asking yourself some questions is necessary: What goals have I established for myself? Can those goals be accomplished where I am? If not, this should be reason enough for you to press toward greater things. Another question one should ask is how does this current state effect those around me? Although you may be physically present, there is a chance that you could be mentally and spiritually absent. If you are not in the right mental and spiritual state, how beneficial is your presence? Once you have gained the motivation to move, it is time to put thoughts into action. Regardless of how long you have been low, going higher should never seem impossible. If you can think it, you can achieve it.

As you push and pull through, remember that he who has begun a good work in you will perform it until the day of Jesus Christ (Philippians 1:6). It doesn't matter where you are right now, God is still working and moving on your behalf; it is your responsibility to believe and trust that he will work everything out in your favor.

# Key Points

# **Key Points**

# Maneuvering Through

*For I the Lord thy God will hold thy right hand, saying
unto thee, Fear not; I will help thee.*

*Isaiah 41:13*

Have you ever experienced something and the wind was
literally knocked out of you? I'm talking about
emotional, mental, or even spiritual situations that hit
you and you can literally feel the effects physically—
tribulations that make you want to give up on life
because "this" can't be what you were created for.
However, regardless of how difficult the situation may
be, you understand that you have to press on through
because things can't end for you in disarray.

When we encounter troubles in our lives, we sometimes
find it hard to keep moving in spite of what we are
facing. Most times it seems as if we are going nowhere
fast. We take five steps forward and get knocked ten
steps back. For every good day we have, we can
guarantee that there will be three bad days. We try our
best to be optimistic, but fear eludes us. As we make our
way through what appears to be a dark tunnel, we see a

light flickering only to find that it was a candle that's no longer lit.

Someway somehow, we have to maneuver through life although we do not have the strength or the energy. Somehow we have to use what we face as a stepping stone to get to where we are going because we can't stay where we are. But how do we move? How do we keep going when life has placed a weight on us that seems way too heavy to bear? How do we keep pressing forward when everything is pulling us back? How do we maneuver through when we don't even know where we are going?

To maneuver through means to move skillfully or carefully. If we are going to maneuver through the hardships of life, we have to do so skillfully and carefully. We need to have a plan. Strategic planning is important. While we will never know the unexpected things that may hit us along the way, a plan gives us a foundation and the ability to get started.

Do not be surprised if you go through your hardships alone. The majority of your difficulties will be dealt with by you and you alone. Rarely will you find someone who is willing to pick up your baggage and help you carry it. Understand that people do not mind helping you sort through your baggage because they can point out flaws and tell you what's wrong with you in the process. But to help you carry the load means to meet you where you are and agree to help you along the way.

I see maneuvering through as us walking through a dark tunnel with little lighting. We are tip toeing as if not to scare anyone while constantly checking our surroundings. I see maneuvering through as us deciding to continue on despite the fact that we do not know where we are going. When it comes to this critical step in one's life, faith must rise up and fear must concede to it. They both cannot take precedence over your life.

Maneuvering through can involve many feelings and emotions, but it is important that you have control over your emotions so that your emotions do not take control over you. It is easy to get caught up in what we feel and see, and sometimes these feelings and emotions are enough to make you want to quit because the process is so unbearable. But it is the process that makes you into who you are supposed to be. It is the process that prepares you for what you have been expecting. Regardless of how hard it will be, press through because God is with you to lead the way. Although you may feel as if you are alone, remember that in Deuteronomy 31:6, God promises to never leave or forsake us.

Change your outlook on what you're dealing with and you will find that the process will not be as difficult. You will discover that the process is actually not against you, but it is working and aligning things in your favor. It is easy for us to become so consumed in how things look that we forget why we are enduring the tests and trials in the first place. The reality is that if we can make it through the process, we show ourselves worthy of the promise. Unfortunately there are no shortcuts to this thing. If we want it, we will have to endure every step to get it. No one wants the process to be longer than what it needs to be, so be sure that you are properly positioned to receive the blessings that belong to you. Make sure you are hearing God's voice and not trying to make your own desires godly. This is enough to prolong the process and create more battles for yourself.

When we shift our thinking, we do not allow the process of maneuvering through our struggles to get the best of us. When we shift our thinking, we put ourselves in a position where we will not allow what we are facing to dominate us but rather, we dominate it, reminding our troubles of the very thing God has promised us. When we can speak life into our situation and relay the message of the promise to the turmoil in our lives, we set ourselves up to be victorious. We set ourselves up to come out a conqueror despite what it may look like at the present moment.

All it takes is a change in our thinking to change our position. Many of us are where we are because we have been bound to the thoughts of defeat. But if we would get control of our thoughts and cast down every thought that does not line up with the will of God for our lives, we could make way for the promise to reign. Unfortunately, none of us have a timetable on how long the process will last. Because of this one simple fact, it is important that we pay special attention to the things that transpire during the season of maneuvering through.

As time goes on, we will undoubtedly become stronger. The very thing that used to weigh you down, you will find does not seem to bother you as much now that you have endured the process a little while. This is what God expects of us as we maneuver through the hardships of life. God wants us to become stronger and better; this is the only way we prove to him we are ready to come out and conquer our next level. In case you did not know, the process of going through is so that you can make it to the other side of what God has for you. Maneuvering through helps us to move from the spoken word to the manifestation. It helps us get from point A to point B.

Let's dig into the three steps of how we can be certain that we are properly maneuvering through:

## Step 1: God Speaks

First, God speaks, and it is very important that we hear what God has said clearly so we know what move we should make next, or if we should even move at all. While all three steps are important, how you react at this point is most important. Has God ever said something that you did not necessarily like? How about God speaking something that goes completely against what you actually want? God supplies all of our needs according to his riches in glory (Philippians 4:19). So when we step aside and disregard our wants, we make room for God to shower down and meet every single one of our needs. So what you do now determines how smoothly the next step goes.

## Step 2: Get Through the Process

We must be receptive to what God is saying even when it doesn't make sense to us. Keeping Isaiah 55:9 in mind, we will constantly remember that God's ways are higher than our ways, and his thoughts are higher than our thoughts. This is encouragement enough to know that although we may not understand God's instruction, he will make things happen so that we come out on top.

The question then becomes, how much do you trust God? Do you trust him enough to follow his instruction even when you are not sure where it will lead? A question that requires much more thought and self-evaluation is, what is your expectation of your own life? When we understand that God always has greater for us, there should be no reason why we reject something so grand. When we take into consideration what God has for us (as if we can come up with something better), we should then wonder why we became complacent with the mediocracy that our lives have handed us. When did wanting God's best become too much for us to desire? What is your expectation of yourself? When we recognize who we really are and who God created us to be, his voice and his instruction becomes so much clearer.

We have been discussing the process of maneuvering through, but we have to be careful that we do not get stuck in the process. The process is difficult and sometimes giving up really does look like the better option. However, we must be committed to making it to the finish line. As the process progresses, it is necessary to stay in constant communication with God.

Understand this one thing: during the process, you are in a very vulnerable place and the enemy recognizes this, so he is strategically seeking whom he may devour (1 Peter 5:8) and that whom is you. He is waiting for you to get discouraged so that he can whisper lies in your ears.

He is waiting for you to get tired so that he does not have to work so hard to make you quit. In case you did not know, the enemy is aware of your promised place too, and it scares him. If you make it to your promised place, the enemy knows that every plan that he has in mind will not prosper (although we know that no weapon formed will prosper anyway, Isaiah 54:17). So while you are going through the process, he's trying his best to get you down. Most times, the enemy recognizes your potential before you. He has a sneak peek of where you are going and who you will become. Because of this, he is battling you. He knows that if you reach your full potential in God, his kingdom will not be able to stand. But as long as you keep your eyes to the hills from which cometh your help (Psalm 121:1), you will not be defeated.

## Step 3: Manifestation

The only way to reach this point is to first adhere to the instruction of God, then to make it through the process. While these may be difficult steps to conquer, you must remember that God graced us for each and every battle that we will face. He has already given us the strength and the formula to succeed; we just need to adhere to what he has told us and we will begin to see things fall into place.

The most difficult thing to do when you are in the middle of distress is to catch your footing. Staying afloat and catching your balance can be challenging when you really have no idea about what is going on around you. Most times, a trial can appear as an unfamiliar environment. Regardless of how many times you may experience hardships, the land of tribulation can always look foreign. Here is what we must grab ahold of: if the land of tribulation does not appear to be foreign to us, we will be okay with living in a place that we were supposed to move through, not settle in and unpack.

Identifying that this is a foreign place should push you through so you can move forward. Going backwards in an attempt to avoid this foreign environment should not be an option. Keep in mind that the only way out is by going through.

When you are going through a tough time, it may be difficult to determine if you should move or remain standing still. Many times, it may seem that during our darkest hours, God is the quietest. It seems that when we need him the most, we cannot hear from him.

How do you maneuver through when there seems to be silence from the one who was supposed to give you specific instructions? How do you maneuver through when it seems as if God has not spoken a word to you? The reality is that we are in an uncomfortable place already and are almost desperate to get out; as a result, we go to extremes so that our turmoil can end. When we get to this point and it appears that God is saying nothing, we should be certain to rely on a previous word that God has spoken to us.

What we do not always realize is that when God speaks to us, we should hold onto those words and use them later on down the line when our lives appear to be going haywire. The words that God speaks to us to pull us through do not expire. They are multi-season words that can apply to many areas of our lives at many different times. The question now becomes, have you kept record of what God has told you? When the going becomes a little too hard as you are maneuvering through your struggle, recall that God says he is always with us.

When we feel that we are experiencing silence from God, we inquire and try to figure out how we are to move with no direction. Consider traveling: Before starting your journey, you enter the address of your destination into your GPS. As you begin the journey, somewhere along the way, you may make a wrong turn or a road may be closed that forces you to go in a direction that your GPS did not anticipate. Automatically, the GPS will begin to reroute but every so often, the GPS loses its way, and is unable to give you further directions.

This is how maneuvering through can appear. You thought you knew where you were going, then something suddenly happens and you realize that you are lost. In this event, you usually will not turn around and return home but rather, you resort to the next best thing of stopping and asking someone for directions. When was the last time you found yourself in the middle of a dark place and you stopped to ask God for directions? So many times, we jump into panic mode instead of remaining calm and simply asking for directions. We believe that because we are lost, we cannot be found. As a result of panicking for so long, when we finally do ask for directions, we cannot hear them because our minds are already cluttered with the confusion that we have exposed ourselves to.

This is why maneuvering through becomes so difficult to do. When we cannot silence the unnecessary noise, we begin to give our attention to the wrong things—the things that ultimately deter and pull us away from where we should be going. While maneuvering through can be challenging, it is possible to do. Fix your eyes on where you are going and not where you currently are. If you can look ahead and not be distracted by your current location, you are guaranteed to reach your promised land.

Let's consider the GPS again. Once you have asked for directions and you have reached a place that is recognizable by your GPS, you will see that it will consider where you are and pick up where it left off. Just like in your spiritual walk, when you have gathered yourself and have proceeded on the right track, you will notice that you are still on your way to your purposed place. Your circumstance is stretching you and as you push through the process, be determined not to quit for quitters cannot reach their promised place.

# Key Points

# **Key Points**

# But Wait... I Thought It Was Over

*We are troubled on every side, yet not distressed; we are perplexed, but not in despair; persecuted, but not forsaken; cast down, but not destroyed.*

*2 Corinthians 4:8-9*

One of the most discouraging times is when you are going through something, things begin to look better and then suddenly, things seem to retreat back to their original state. This is enough to drive one crazy. You believe that things have gotten better in your life and that things are turning around and out of nowhere, it seems that you end up right back where you started. It is almost as if everything you have dedicated yourself to has been a waste because the ending seems to be a duplication of the beginning.

Experiencing the same thing again can be challenging, but this is a time when you should identify what could have possibly caused this turn of events. This would be the time to identify the hurdles in our lives. Merriam-Webster defines a hurdle as an artificial barrier over which racers must leap. To go even deeper, artificial is defined as man-made. If you think about a runner on a track field, when they come to a hurdle, the goal is to jump over it and continue with the race. However, there may come a time every now and again when one is not able to make it over the hurdle. As a result, the runner gets hurt and/or the hurdle is knocked down.

The only way the runner is able to jump over the hurdle is if they recognize that it is there. What hurdles are in your life that you have failed to recognize? Not recognizing hurdles and leaping over them only leaves us hurt and slows us down. The hurdle that is slowing you down is man-made—something that you have created on your own. What self-made barriers have you brought into your life? It is time that we identify the hurdles so that we can remove them and proceed on the path to destiny.

The thing about hurdles is that they may be things or even people we favor. In this case, leaping over and leaving behind things and people as you proceed with your journey will not be an easy task. But what if the reoccurrence of feelings, events, and circumstances were directly related to the hurdles that you have grown to love? While many times we would rather not admit it, those things that we are attached to can sometimes be the things that hold us captive to our present state. We have heard the saying, "Everything that is good to you, may not be good for you." This explains that just because we have a passion for something, that does not necessarily mean it has a passion for us in return.

How are you willing to deal with the possible hurdles in your life? Are you willing to identify those hurdles and remove them? Or would you rather keep them around and continuously trip and fall over them? At some point, we have to release self-injurious behavior and take the necessary steps so that we can boldly walk into the next dimension of life.

The thing about the enemy is that he does not try new tricks. He comes with the same thing in a different way; and if we are not careful, we will fall for what he has done and will not even realize that it is the same thing that he tried in the last season. It is very important that we position ourselves by being alert so that we can identify when the enemy is trying to set us up for his plan of distraction and ultimately, destruction. The thing about the enemy is that he comes with what you like.

Consider the hurdles that were mentioned, the enemy will present you with the things that you desire the most; and if you are oblivious to his tactics, you will seek after your desire, not realizing it was a distraction in disguise. If we are aware of when he shows up, then we are more able to stop him before he has the chance to fully set his plan into motion.

Here is the thing about the adversary: he will go inch by inch. The more leeway you give him, the more leeway he will take. If you allow him to get away with one thing, he will try for two. If you are not careful, before you know it, you will have let him in and given him more than he should have ever had to begin with. This is why you must be familiar with his tricks so that you can recognize them from the moment they present themselves to you. If you see these schemes from the beginning, then you put yourself in a position to conquer them when they come your way.

What we must understand is that we can outsmart the enemy. He only has as much power as we give him; if we allow him to cause fear in our lives, he will take advantage of our fearful state and continue to do what he has already started and more. However, if we speak to his tricks and tactics and command them to return back to the very pits of hell where they belong, we can stop him in his tracks. James 4:7 tells us that if we submit ourselves to God and resist the devil, then he will flee from us. So we cannot entertain what he brings and then expect him to leave when we are ready for him to go. We must make up in our minds from the very beginning that we will not give any energy to the ways of the enemy. The more energy we invest in him, the more energy he will invest in us. He will feed off of what we do when he comes knocking on our doors.

Entertaining what the enemy presents can be done in two different ways: by cracking under pressure or by going along with his games. If we crack under pressure, we have given the enemy our vulnerability and the free will to do whatever he wants with it. He is already testing you, but once he sees how it affects you, he then has more ingredients to add to his formula to destroy you. On the other hand, if we willingly participate in his tactics, we show him that we have time to spend on his playground, and he will want us to stay longer than we ever intended. Once we arrive to his playground and begin to participate in his games, we either find more things that spark our interest or we find it difficult to leave. Can you see how deciding to take interest in the games of the enemy will result in no good in the end?

Remember that regardless of what the enemy may bring your way, you have power over him. And because you have power over him, don't forfeit that power and give it to him. This only positions you beneath him when you were created to defeat him. When you hand over your power, you then leave yourself powerless; and how can you fight if you have given your strength away? God created you in his image and with a plan in mind. Do not sacrifice that plan because you would rather give the enemy power over you. God has anointed you for a specific reason, and the enemy cannot kill what God has put life into.

Most of the time when we find ourselves going in a direction that appears to be backwards, we wonder if we missed a lesson or an opportunity that has caused a detour. What I have learned is that sometimes detours keep us from getting too relaxed on our journey and prevents us from falling asleep. I am reminded of the story of Eutychus in the book of Acts. Falling asleep resulted in death for him but by the miraculous power of God, he was brought back to life. While this story and others in the Bible display the resurrection power of Jesus, God wants us to realize that we do not have to die in order to experience a miracle. Sometimes he will allow detours so that we do not fall asleep and miss important details along the way. Be mindful that God knows all. He knows the roads we will take before we even head in a particular direction. However, God does not desire to put us in harm's way. We may find that God will redirect our choices with a detour to keep us awake and to keep us from traveling down a road that could put us to sleep.

In 2018, we are now experiencing a time when people are encouraged to "stay woke" when it comes to racial injustice across the country. Everyone is encouraged to keep their eyes open and acknowledge the injustices that occur. Making Black history a part of everyday lives and giving honor to our predecessors is the norm for many. Just like this, it is important to "stay woke" so that we do not begin to accept the tricks the enemy throws our way.

While it may seem that you are back at square one, realize that it may not be square one after all—it could be preparation for the next level in disguise. Your struggle may seem never-ending but remember that if there was a beginning that guarantees that an ending is in the future. All things must come to an end, but better is the ending. Avoiding the cycle of regression is possible if you commit yourself to moving forward and not going back regardless of what may come your way. Commit yourself to the future and leave the past where it ended.

You will be able to avoid the cycle when you are no longer moved by the things of that past. Be intentional about not falling into traps that are dedicated to positioning themselves in the way of your progress. Remain focused on your journey because it is only a test; and whether you believe it or not, you have what it takes to handle hard times that may come after you have experienced triumph.

Have you reached the point where you truly believe that you can come out of what it is that you're experiencing? Many times we half believe that God can do something but expect full results. What do I mean? Well, we do not have full confidence that God can work things out for us, yet we expect God to perform a miracle on our behalf. In order to see manifestations of what God has promised us, we have to believe that they will actually come to pass. We must put in the effort and meet God halfway to show him that we are serious and will do whatever it takes to experience a supernatural move from him. Many times, we are not waiting on God; he is actually waiting for us to perfect our posture so we are in place to receive what he has for us.

Oftentimes, we become so caught up in what we see that we disregard what God has already done for us. What if your battle is already over and God is recapping where he has brought you from? He is giving you flashes of where you have been so you can recall every single blessing he has given to you over the course of your trial. The truth is, we tend to forget that God has met our needs once those needs have been met. It is almost as if we are never satisfied. Once God does one thing, we are ready for the next. Do we ever take time to just bask in the goodness that he has already given to us? More times than not, we get caught up in the big things and forget about the small things that God has done. We must realize that the small blessings God has rendered were only preparing us for the bigger blessings that he had in store. If it had not been for the small things, we would not be worthy of the bigger things.

If we find that we seem to have regressed instead of progressed, we should keep in mind that God is not taking us back to hurt us but rather, he is using our past to serve as a reminder. Now the question becomes, can you withstand the reminder? The moment of the reminder is not the time to throw in the towel. This is the time for you to rejoice over where you have come from. Are you able to identify your growth and how far you have come? Taking note of your progress and process is how you can recover when it seems that you have backtracked.

There are some times when you just have to get over it. There may be times when God will bring the same situation back around full circle so that you no longer have a tolerance for it and can no longer accept it. After a while, you are over it and because you are over it, you no longer have the desire to deal with it. Have you reached the point where you are over the situation that you have been dealing with for so long? Sometimes, God will allow us to experience the same thing not so that it can destroy us, but so that we can become tired of it and leave it alone. God does not always want to take things away from us and remove them from our lives; he will sometimes give us the authority to do the moving ourselves. He wants us to realize who and what we need. Before moving forward, God may need to know if you are tapped into your future enough to know who can stay and who needs to go. So, yes, you thought it was over; but you still had a desire for that old thing and in order to successfully move forward, you have to remove yourself from the things that mean you no good.

There is always the possibility that God may have brought you back to the situation so that you can realize you don't need what you desired after all. God may have brought you back to the situation so that you realize that you are capable of living without it. How many times have we attached ourselves to things or people because we believe that we need them in our lives, not realizing that God has already provided us the things that we need to make it through? Don't become so attached to what looks good that you forget what you actually need.

Everything that glitters isn't gold; we all know the saying, but we need to make it relevant to our lives. Every person who looks good may not be the person who is supposed to take up space in our lives. Every job that pays well may not be the job that you are supposed to be employed at. We have to release ourselves from the "feel good" and attach ourselves to the things that put us in pursuit of our destiny.

Are you ready to release all of the dead weight and attach yourself to things that promote life? It may not be easy to do in the beginning; but once you release the things that mean you no good in life, things become better all of a sudden. Hard situations are not as hard because you have the right things and the right people attached to you. The trials you face are not so difficult because you have the right circle surrounding you and ensuring you can make it. When we are tired of the same thing and we are over it, then we can progress, move forward, and begin to conquer the road of becoming who we are destined to be.

Be sure that you are not fighting with conditions. What does that mean? That translates to us wanting to be winners but simultaneously dragging along the things that influence us to lose. We must choose. Do we want to be conquerors or do we want to settle for what makes us comfortable?

# Key Points

# Key Points

# I Was Made for This

*For the Lord your God is he that goeth with you, to fight*
*for you against your enemies, to save you.*

*Deuteronomy 20:4*

The most enlightening moment during a struggle is when you realize that you have what it takes to win. It is kind of like the quote that says, "There are two important days in a person's life: the day they are born and the day they find out why." It is almost as if you discover purpose all over again within the storm. You have a new confidence when you realize that you do not have to be bound to what you are experiencing. New confidence causes us to walk differently; and think of how intimidating it is to the adversary when you develop a new stride that will ultimately work against him.

When the battle you are in was orchestrated, God knew you would win before it even began. First Corinthians 10:13 tells us that God won't put more on us than we can bear. Knowing this, we are reminded that God would not put us in something that we could not handle. Think about this: sometimes God will place us in the middle of a crisis—not to hurt us but to expose us to our own strength. How would you know that you have what it takes to win if you are never put in a predicament that exemplifies your strength? God is teaching you countless things about yourself that you would not have known had you not gone through certain things.

"Experience is the best teacher," not only the best teacher about life, but the best teacher about you. What would you know about yourself if you never had to fight a battle? How would you know that you could win if you never stepped in the ring? In the end, you become wise enough to know that you can utilize tools that God has given you in other areas to assist you as you pull through your current struggle.

These battles we encounter are strategically created. God looks at the battle and he looks at us; and as if in comparison of strength, he ensures that we have the ability to survive it if we are put in the battle. Can you believe that God sets us up to win, even the battles that seem to be whipping the life out of us? Regardless of how trying it may be or how defeated you may feel, God still designed the battle for you to win. We have the upper hand in these situations but if we fail to recognize this, we become stagnant and risk forfeiting the strength that we have been given.

In the sixth chapter of Ephesians, we learn about the full armor of God. If you did not know, this alone puts you in position to win as long as you make the proper use of each article included in the armor. The scripture instructs us to put on the whole armor of God so that we may be able to stand against the wiles of the devil (Ephesians 6:11). What we must remember is that it is necessary to wear the armor in its entirety. We cannot pick and choose which part of the armor we want to wear and expect to successfully come up against the adversary. So we must understand the purpose of each piece of the armor. When we understand the purpose, we are more easily able to apply these articles and make proper use of them.

We start with the belt of truth. Are you able to separate the lies in your life from the truth that God has spoken to you and over you? We must be able to rely on the truth even when things around us go against everything that we know. The breastplate of righteousness is placed close to our hearts. Why, you may wonder. To be righteous means to be morally right or justifiable. The breastplate of righteousness is a matter concerning the condition of your heart. Is your heart right and are your actions justifiable in the sight of God? We should have the gospel of peace on our feet so that as we go through tough times, we have the peace of God directing us and keeping us in our right minds. The shield of faith gives us what we need to cancel out the doubt that the enemy may try to throw our way. He understands that battles can be overwhelming for us, so he never misses an opportunity to shake us up. The shield of faith prepares us so that we can beat the enemy at his own game. The helmet of salvation is so important because it protects our beliefs and coordination as it relates to our faith. Without salvation, what would be the point in striving to live a life that's pleasing in God's eyes? Our salvation is the foundation of our walk with Christ, and we should protect it by all means. When times get difficult we can use our sword and speak the word of God to the adversary. "Thy word have I hid in mine heart, that I might not sin against thee" (Psalm 119:11). This verse gives great counsel on how to keep our sword readily available and near. Whenever hardships arise, we should be able to rely on the word that lives in us, using our sword to cast down imagination and every high thing that exalts itself against the knowledge of God (2 Corinthians 10:5).

"Have you considered my servant Job? (Job 1:8)" The first chapter in the Book of Job takes us through the journey of how the enemy selected Job for the trial that we have heard of so many times. Job had everything but he lost everything; and in the end, because he was faithful to God even in the midst of what he had to endure, he got back everything and more. Before the enemy can attack you, he must first get permission from God. The first chapter of Job gives us the exchange between God and the enemy. The enemy was roaming the earth and in a sense, looking for his next victim. This reminds me of 1 Peter 5:8: "your adversary the devil, as a roaring lion, walketh about, seeking whom he may devour." While the enemy is seeking his next target, we should be getting suited in the armor because we never know when he is going to attack. When we are suited, we prepare ourselves for what is to come, even if we do not see it coming. The first part of 1 Peter 5:8 tells us to be sober and vigilant. When the enemy comes, he comes strong; and if we are not ready, we risk being defeated in a fight that we have the capability to win. The enemy will not take it easy on you, so don't take it easy on him!

Going back to Job, the enemy was roaming the earth and the Lord begins to converse with him. As the dialogue progresses, the Lord asked the enemy if he had considered testing Job. This may be hard to understand, but God orchestrated this battle for Job because he knew that Job possessed the necessary tools to win. Verse one tells us that Job was blameless, upright, feared God, and shunned evil. Because of his character, he had what it would take to defeat the enemy in his attempt to take him out. How does your character represent you? Can your character uphold you in a battle? We must examine who we are behind closed doors, because that is the person the enemy is coming after. If we are fit and in shape, we can take on the wiles of the enemy that come our way.

The most unfortunate thing would be leaving a storm the same way you went in. Imagine going through something and at the end, you still think the same and walk the same. Struggles have a way of breaking you without leaving you broken. As God is breaking you, he is simultaneously building you back up so that at no point are you left empty. Because of this very reason, the beginning of the fight should have no indication of how things will end. After all, Ecclesiastes 7:8 tells us "better is the end of a thing than the beginning". Who you were in the beginning should not reflect who you are once the battle is over.

What would be the point of all the pain endured if at the end, there was no growth? God does not take us through storms only for us to exit them in the same shape in which we entered. It is almost as if God puts us in a position where growth is mandatory. What would be the consequences of still being the same person you were when you first fell to your knees in your fight? How would you conquer the adversary of your next level if you were only in shape to deal with the adversaries of your current level? Once we develop a mindset of greater, we become desperate for change. And if obtaining change requires us to go through heartaches, headaches, and emotional pain we make a conscious decision to endure because we realize that in the end, it will be better.

One thing we must be intentional about doing is noting our progress as we go along. Don't wait until the end of a thing to praise yourself for your courage. Rather, look at each battle individually and realize how you have made it beyond situations that should have left you broken. When you begin to acknowledge the small steps, you will notice your progress and recognize and believe that if the last battle did not break you, then you have the ability and the strength to win the next battle when it arrives. One of our biggest mistakes is that we tend to be too hard on ourselves and do not give ourselves the credit that we deserve. Being better than yesterday is still improvement even if it is a little.

Instead of looking at a battle piece by piece, we tend to look at the big picture; and when we do not see things coming together, we are convinced that what we see is all there is or all we will ever be. When we look in the mirror and change how we view ourselves, then we will begin to see how we are no longer who we used to be.

And once we see this change, we can begin to speak this change. Once we begin to speak the changes that we see, we deposit positive affirmations about ourselves into the atmosphere, and this simple task commands our environment to change and become subject to that which we have spoken.

Usually, we won't realize our strength until we are put in a position to use it. Times such as this require us to take a look at who we really are; and when that takes place, we can recite and believe that we can do all things through Christ who gives us strength (Philippians 4:13), because we were made for the fight and created to win.

What if when we entered the battle, we could find all the ways that we can win and not fall victim to thinking that we will lose from the beginning? Have you ever heard of the saying, "How you start it is how you finish"? Well, if we start in a defeated state, then it is likely that we will end in the same way. Now, understand that you can develop a change of heart and a change of mind and because of this, the outcome can drastically change. But if we go into what we have to deal with knowing that we are already more than conquerors (Romans 8:37), then it is so much easier to fight the battle.

When we have the mentality of a winner, we then act like winners; and when we begin to act like winners, we ultimately will become winners. If we have plans on winning, we cannot move in defeat. Defeat starts in the mind and if we do not control our defeated thoughts, then we will act in a defeated manner. The enemy wants for you to have a defeated mind because if you think defeat, you will speak defeat. And soon, those thoughts will become actions.

We must be cautious of the thoughts that we allow to take up residence in our minds. When we make room for one thought, we ultimately make room for more to grow. If we are not careful, those thoughts could potentially consume us to the point where we begin to believe them. Although you may not necessarily be defeated, constantly thinking defeat will cause manifestations in ways you never knew could be possible. It saddens me that most times, we count ourselves out before the battle even begins. We become so intimidated by what we see that we forget who we were made to be; we forget who we were created by.

God created us in his image. That automatically gives us the strength to endure and the strength to win. Think about it: God sent his Son to die for us, and still we disobey, disregard, and sometimes show no concern for him. Wouldn't you think that hurts God to witness how we behave? Yet in spite of that, he still shows us his sovereignty, his power, and his strength. As a matter of fact, he even sent his power to dwell within us by way of the Holy Spirit. This is enough power to conquer anything that may come our way.

We possess the necessary strength to make it through whatever we encounter; it is simply up to us to believe in that strength when it comes time to use it. We cannot be afraid to utilize our strength because when we are fearful to use what we have, we do not use it to its full capacity. As a result, we do not apply strength when and where it's needed and ultimately, we set ourselves up to fail. Do you actually have an idea of what you were made for? It is easy to say yes but if we have no idea of our true ability, then we are merely just stating words that have no real meaning behind them. The title of this chapter is "I Was Made for This," but can you properly identify what you were made for? Do you know what your "this" is? Do you know where it developed and how? What is the root cause of what you are facing? If you find it challenging to recognize what it is that you have to face, how can you successfully enter the battle?

Identifying the adversary is so important in winning because you must be able to know who you are fighting. What would it be to learn that you have fought a battle that wasn't even yours? What if you learned that you have slayed a giant that wasn't even after you? If we are not careful with who we jump into a battle with, we may find that we have used our energy and become distracted by something that never had intentions on distracting us.

What are you fighting? Have you rightfully identified who you should be going up against? When we say that we are made for something, we adopt a certain confidence that positions us to take it on because we go in believing that we have what it takes to conquer. Once we can consider what we are fighting, we are now in a position to fight accordingly. You cannot fight every adversary in the same way. What may defeat one, may not work for the next. Consider this: Ways of escape in your last season could very well be things that lead you to turmoil in this season. Understand that old ways cannot open new doors. The enemy is slick; he will present you with things that helped you before, and he will force you to believe that they will bring you out again. All the while, he's setting a trap and if you aren't careful, you could run into it.

What does winning mean to you? Are you content with simply knocking your giant down or are you in the mindset of ensuring he does not get back up? Your definition of winning will determine how hard you fight and what you do once the battle is over. Does your determination influence you to fight until you are sure there is no more life left in your giant? Or will you become tired midway and settle for whatever results you see? When we acknowledge what winning really is and what winning really means to us, we can fight differently. It is almost as if we see the purpose behind it; and because we understand the "why," we can react accordingly. Understanding that we were made not only for the fight, but also to win the fight gives us a confidence that is needed to be victorious upon the start of our battle.

You must realize that you were anointed to win. The reality is that everyone can fight, but not everyone is positioned to win. Fighting is actually the easy part. Withstanding what you have to encounter is where your ground can get shaken. Even on shaky ground, we have the ability to stand up straight, stand up tall, and develop a balance that will help us stand strong even in the most crucial situations.

# Key Points

# **Key Points**

_____

_____

_____

_____

_____

_____

_____

_____

_____

_____

_____

_____

_____

_____

_____

_____

_____

_____

_____

_____

# Piecing Things Together

*And we know that all things work together for good to
them that love God, to them who are the called
according to his purpose.*

*Romans 8:28*

The good thing about being broken is that you now have
the formula to piece yourself together. The formula is
simply the pieces lying in front of you; it is only a matter
of putting the puzzle together.

Life is like a puzzle full of small pieces. Consider the
many times that you have come across puzzles in your
life. It is always easier to put together the puzzle with
the bigger pieces. These are the ones that seem to be the
easiest to complete. It takes less time, and it is not so
hard to figure out. We always tend to go for what is
easier over the things that are more challenging because
it's less stressful and less difficult. But in order to grow
and to mature, we sometimes have to make the decision
to choose the more challenging thing. The thing that is
more challenging may very well be the thing that turns
out to be the best for us.

When we begin to understand that easier is not always better, we will stop choosing what is lesser and more convenient. Winners are not birth out of convenience. They are birthed from making a decision in their hearts and minds to accept the challenge regardless of the cost. If you wish to be a winner, you have to be okay with a tussle. You will not come out on top without a fight. The battle is part of the process. Winners will always have to be uncomfortable if they expect to be victorious. The small pieces of your life may be uncomfortable to sort through and time-consuming; but if we wish to be better in the end, we must commit ourselves to the very pieces of the process, even those pieces that stretch us. The stretching produced by being uncomfortable is necessary if we want to be greater in the end.

Piecing things together comes about when understanding is reached. When we can begin to understand that our current place is connected to a greater cause, we do not despise it as much as if we had no understanding at all. Once we "get it," it is as if something automatically clicks. When we realize that things are really not about us, but about how we can reach destiny and fulfill purpose, things do not look so bad.

The small pieces you may encounter could be bitterness, hatred, lust, anger, discontentment, abuse, and broken heartedness, just to name a few. Before piecing these all together, we must be sure that we have addressed and dealt with the pieces individually. Broken and damaged pieces cannot make up the full picture. If we do not handle the small issues before piecing them together, then we are unconsciously preparing for disaster. It would be disheartening to work so hard at fixing what was broken only to learn that in the end, you missed vital steps that only lead to you experiencing brokenness again.

Once we are able to get to a place where we can acknowledge the small pieces and accept them as they are, we can then begin putting the puzzle together. Completing this task will take patience; and if you are not content with the many pieces of the puzzle, you will find that you easily become frustrated. On your journey to wholeness, the enemy will try to distract you and if you are not careful, you may find that you repeatedly fall for his tricks. Yes, wholeness takes work but it is not impossible to achieve.

When you become tired of being broken, you will allow nothing to stand in the way of reaching a healthy state. Healthiness is a necessity for longevity in life, and if our emotional, mental, or spiritual state is not in a place that is conducive to our well-being, then we will find that our physical being is in jeopardy.

Be intentional about understanding the pieces that are set before you. It is less challenging to put a puzzle together when you have an idea of what it should look like. Think of that moment when you are putting a puzzle together and you get stuck. Most of us will look at the packaging to remind ourselves of what we should be working towards. We will begin to look at the pieces and say to ourselves or those with whom we are working, "Here is a foot. It looks like it goes here." And then we begin to organize the pieces in a way that will help us bring the picture together. We know that God's thoughts and plans exceed our own, and because of this, we will never know what exactly God has in store. But if we can put the pieces together so that they displays joy, peace, happiness, and contentment with God's will, then we are piecing things together in a way that will help us along our journey to winning.

This is a crucial step in one's fight because in order to reach this point, you had to endure things that probably seemed unbearable in the beginning. To get to the place where you are ready to piece your life back together takes real courage. Why, you may ask. Well when piecing yourself back together, you must keep in mind that the possibility of being broken again is always in view. One may ask why even piece yourself back together then? Well you can't operate in your fullest potential while in a broken state.

Although the possibility of being broken again may be a given, because you have experienced your broken state, you are now more cautious and careful about the people and things you allow in your space. Because you are aware of what caused such a difficult time in your life, you are intentional about not giving these things precedence in your life. You have taken heed to those individual broken pieces in your life and given them the attention they deserve. This has resulted in healing, and because the small things have healed, that provides a glue that will make it difficult to encounter brokenness again.

Once we stop viewing brokenness as a bad thing, we can finally realize the good that can actually come from it. While it is not a bad thing, it is not a place where we should remain. We should strive to be better than who we are at the current moment. Out of brokenness comes strength. Sometimes we don't recognize our true strength until we are broken and have to figure out how to move from where we are. We may be in predicaments where our strength through God is the only way out. If we do not tap into it, we find that we will remain in the shape we are in; however, none of us desire to stay in the same broken condition. If we were to tell the truth, being broken does not feel good.

From brokenness, courage can develop. Being at your lowest somehow has a way of giving you courage that you never thought you could obtain. It is almost like the flight, fight, and freeze reaction. If you are not familiar with this response, it is when we are in dangerous situations or any situation that causes panic, and we can either flee from the situation, fight the situation, or freeze in the situation. Finding courage is an example of fighting the situation. With courage, you can develop what it will take to overcome whatever you are in.

Being broken is a time when someone discovers who he or she really is. Brokenness has a way of forcing you to be better the next time around. This is why we never go back to who we once were when we've truly experienced brokenness. It's almost like an awakening that is far too painful to endure twice. Can you consider the last time you faced something that literally changed your life forever? We never want to endure hardships twice but some hardships hit us harder than others; and at the end, we make up in our minds that no matter what life brings down the line, *this* one thing we will not allow to happen again.

Broken things have purpose. That purpose is simply to become whole so that a greater calling can be answered. What broken pieces in you serve a greater cause, but lie dormant because you won't give it the attention that it deserves? Don't be afraid to fiddle and play with your broken pieces. Learn those pieces. Learn what caused that brokenness. Learn it so that you can never be broken for that same reason again.

While it may have hurt, brokenness was never intended to actually hurt you. It just wanted to make you better. Here's the thing about brokenness: it probably didn't even know that it was creating a masterpiece. If the enemy knew that his tricks were actually grooming us for what God has for us, he would think twice before he came our way. He seeks to destroy us but what he does not realize is that with God on our side, we have the power within us to destroy what he intended to use to destroy us. Do not allow the enemy to hold you captive to what he has in mind for you. We must learn to find the good in what hurt us instead of becoming captive to it and living as a victim. When we find the good, we eliminate room for the bad that could possibly occur.

So how do we actually piece things together? Well, first observation and identification must take place. Recognize what caused the brokenness to begin with, whether it be a bad relationship, making wrong choices, or some other circumstance that caused a life dilemma. If you can identify what caused the problem, you are on your way to defeating it so that there is never a next time.

Identifying the problem alone is not enough. You must go deeper than that. If we identify the cause but make no attempt at changing the cause, this process will not be worthwhile. So after identifying the problem, we must discover the specifics that caused the problem. This is so important because if we only identify the problem, but not the characteristics of the problem that actually caused the damaged, we risk facing the same problem in different environments.

Don't piece things back together so that they look the same as before. What would be the point of trials if they never changed us? Expect the outcome to be different. Expect to think differently. Expect to have a different perspective. Expect the things that used to bother you to suddenly not matter anymore. When we expect differently than what we have seen, we make room for God to show up in our lives and do the unexpected.

Brokenness can be painful but even still, there lies a lesson: The aftermath should enlighten you on what it takes to break you apart. You become more self-aware because you have discovered a new part of yourself that you have not acknowledged in the past. You find self-worth; there is something about brokenness that opens your eyes to who you truly are. Brokenness will cause you to see yourself in a light that you have overlooked for whatever reason. Sometimes, God has to break us to show us the diamond that we really are. If you know anything about diamonds, then you know that they go through a strenuous process in order to reach their final state. They do not start as those shiny jewels that everyone loves. They go through a process and develop into what we know them to be. Just like the diamond, we have to endure a long, strenuous process that in the end causes us to be the top pick!

How many times have our minds become clouded with who we think we are? False identity is deadly, and there will be times when God has to break us in order to loose us from the spirit of who we think we are. We create in our minds who we wish to be, and we adapt a persona of someone who does not coincide to whom God has called us to be. When was the last time you conducted self-reflection and admitted to yourself that who you saw in the mirror was not the same person God had created in his image?

Piecing things together will always be necessary. The struggle with this is understanding that broken things still have purpose. It does not matter where you are or where you have been. Your broken pieces are part of the puzzle, and they are just as relevant as who you are when you are whole. Those pieces are what make you who you are. Do not resent those broken pieces but rather, do what is needed to make them whole. We tend to become caught up in what brokenness looks like. We count ourselves out based on where we are, not realizing that God can and will use broken people. Being broken does not disqualify us from God's love; it perfectly positions us so that we can experience it and know that it was nothing but the love of God that could have possibly put a broken person back together again. God has the capability to put broken things back together and make them beautiful.

Not understanding your purpose while in a broken place does not make your purpose less purposeful. Purpose cannot be erased because of where we are. When God calls us, he does not change his mind. We are the ones who operate against purpose and then find ourselves in hurtful places. However, in spite of that, we should still be able to see that we are stronger than what we once were. You may wonder how you can piece yourself together. Well, the reality is that we should leave the mending up to God.

We are too fragile and most times we don't even know how to handle ourselves with care; and consequently, we cause more damage when our intent was only to put ourselves back together again. This is mainly because we tend to do what feels good in the moment, but we neglect things that are beneficial to our future. When we turn ourselves over to God, we allow him to perform surgery and fix broken places that we didn't even know existed. God is the ultimate mender and when he puts us back together, he ensures that we will never be broken in such a way again.

We should keep in mind that we still have a responsibility that includes not returning to familiar places. Once God puts you back together, be careful not to revert to old habits and environments. At this point, you are vulnerable; and revisiting what has broken you in the past could break you in a way that causes much more damage than before. While you can never be broken beyond repair, why put yourself in a position to experience the same anguish and disappointment again? Old ways will not produce new results, and leading yourself to the same toxic environment will not be beneficial to your growth.

Understand that everyone cannot make it to your future. Be conscious about who you allow in your life. Be intentional about protecting your peace. While this may be a hard pill to swallow, it is necessary to release some things if you wish to survive in your next level. This is the most appropriate time to separate the wheat from the tare. Who among you is as weeds and are no good for you? By now, they have probably exposed themselves so separation should come easy.

This is the time to begin valuing the new you. Adopt new habits that compliment who you are and where you are going. Be careful not to jeopardize the work God has done by sticking with the former things. You are better off now then you were before. Although you may not see it immediately, a change has taken place and old ways will not help you prosper in your new light.

# Key Points

# Key Points

_____

_____

_____

_____

_____

_____

_____

_____

_____

_____

_____

_____

_____

_____

_____

_____

_____

_____

_____

# I Can See the Light

*For our light affliction, which is but for a moment,*
*worketh for us a far more exceeding and eternal weight*
*of glory.*

*2 Corinthians 4:17-18*

Piecing things together and seeing the light are two vital parts of a process. They are different stages and cannot happen simultaneously. In order to progress from one level to the next, one will need to go through internal cleansing. This is not about a physical position but rather, the posture of your heart and the condition of your mind. Reaching a place where you are able to see the light requires honesty about yourself. Can you admit your own shortcomings to yourself? Or do you constantly live in denial about where you are?

Here is the thing about the light: It is always on, but it is up to us when we begin to see it. Once our eyes adjust to our surroundings, then we will notice that the light has been on all along. When we adjust our attitudes and change our thinking, we will notice that what we have been looking for was right in front of our eyes all along.

But in order to see, we must check our vision. A certain level of maturity is needed in order for one to successfully move from one point to the next.

What did not make sense before starts to make sense now. Blind eyes become open and ultimately, you become content with where you are to the point where you act in a way that changes your circumstance. Suddenly, things don't seem as bad anymore. When you are able to see the light, you recognize that the finish line is in view. Regardless of what may be happening around you, you have a determination to focus on the light. The light becomes your motivation to keep moving. It brightens your dark place and brings about hope in what may appear to be a hopeless situation. Most likely, the light you see won't be a physical light, but it could be something as significant as remembering the promise spoken over your life. Recalling the promise will help things around you make sense.

Too many times, we fall victim to the distraction of reality. We allow what we see to affect what we know to be true. Somehow, we always believe the natural over the spiritual although the spiritual will always be the dominant force. Although the pain is natural and tangible, becoming subjective to it does not draw us closer to what we desire to see. In all actuality when we believe what we see over the word we have heard from God himself, we get further from where we need to be. The most common trick of the enemy is making you doubt what God has told you. If you doubt what God has told you, the enemy's job becomes easier.

The first step to seeing the light is believing the word that has been spoken, whether it be directly from the Holy Bible or a unique word just for you. If you do not believe it, you become stagnant in moving towards the manifestation of it. Once we believe, we require our entire being to get on one accord. And when our natural man is on one accord with our spirit man, we can be on one accord with God.

Seeing the light is a decision that we must make. When we become tired of going through the storm and going down the same road, we make up in our minds—whether consciously or unconsciously—that we want to see the light. Consciously can be simply making a declaration, while unconsciously can be an unexpected change in our actions. We may not necessarily announce it with our mouths but somewhere along the line, our perspective begins to change, and then our mindset begins to change, and then we begin to speak differently. And once we deposit words into the atmosphere, our actions change and before we know it, we are living a life in accordance with seeing the light.

I pose this question to you: Can you stand to see the light? When you get to the place where you begin to notice that the light is shining in your life, are you running towards it or are you running away from it? Sometimes we do not know how to react to such a thing. This is truly a turning point; and if we are not careful, we can mistake the light for a distraction, thinking that it is trying to blind us. If you find that you are in an apprehensive space when you begin to see the light, you should be careful because this is exactly what the enemy wants. He wants you to become fearful so that you can turn around and neglect your responsibility to move forward. He would rather you go through the storm and through the rain because he knows that once you take heed and become subjective to the light, he will no longer have power over your way of thinking or your actions.

So if we see the light and we become a little hesitant, we must remember to stay true to God's promise and be committed to finding out what the light is trying to show us. We do not have to remain in our past or who we used to be. We are not obligated to stay the same but we have a responsibility to grow, mature, and learn. When you see that light shining, it is probably in your best interest to see what it's about. Although it may seem as if the light is blinding you, what we must grab ahold of is that the blessing that God has for us is so big, it is so great, it is so mighty that we may have to squint to see it; but we're not squinting because it is too bright, we're squinting because it is so big.

The brightness of the light signifies how God is ready to blow your mind. The big blessing that you have been anticipating and waiting for is just beyond the light. So how do you react when you see the light? This is not the time to give up. This is not the time to go back to what made you comfortable, but this is the time to accept being uncomfortable so that you are in a place where your hands are open and ready to receive what God has for you.

We must get to a point where we stop allowing the devil to make decisions for us. If we see the light, we should attach ourselves to its rays. If we hear victory, we should dance to the music that it brings. No longer should we be content with what the adversary has to say about us. He has no rule, no power, and no dominion over us. Because this is a fact, we can use our God-given power to defeat him so that he may never approach us again, trying to destroy what God has given to us. We have endured entirely too much to give him a show and allow him to take us back to the place that we have struggled to be delivered from.

This point in the process is probably the most profound place you will find yourself: It is a time of enlightenment and you are probably considering the fact that things have not actually been so bad. It is funny how once our heads are above water and we can finally breathe, we realize that what we have endured wasn't the worst after all. Of course while in the midst of the trial, it seems as if we have never experienced anything quite like it. When we get to a point where we can see the bigger picture, in this case, seeing the light, the struggles do not seem like such a big deal anymore.

Upon seeing the light, our goal should be to press towards it until we reach it. Understand that the enemy is frightened by what will happen once you reach your appointed place. So things may not necessarily become easier upon seeing the light, but you develop a little more fight in you that will bring you to your expected end. And because you have more fight that has been built upon your newfound strength, you are able to take shots from the enemy that in the past would have probably knocked you down. I just mentioned a newfound strength, and you may be wondering where that strength has come from. That strength has been developed over the course of your process.

Consider when you first begin working out at the gym. For a person who has never done an intense workout, this will be a challenge. However, as time goes on, you will begin to realize that what was difficult in the beginning is actually extremely easy now. You may actually welcome more challenging workouts because you've realized that you have the ability to do it.

In the same way, when we see the light, we finally take hold of the fact that we have it within us to win whatever we may be facing. We are no longer intimidated by our struggles or the enemy. We are now at a place where we find strength in the light. I'm reminded of John 8:12 where Jesus makes it known that he is the light of the world. When we are looking at the light, we are actually looking at Jesus: The one who is the way, the truth, and the life (John 14:6). And if we look to him, we have no choice but to succeed. When we look to him, we are following the GPS that is set to take us in the right direction. When we look at the light, we avoid the detours, delays, and the distractions that may be set up along the way.

# <u>Key Points</u>

_____
_____
_____
_____
_____
_____
_____
_____
_____
_____
_____
_____
_____
_____
_____
_____
_____
_____
_____

# Key Points

# Now Faith

*Now faith is the substance of things hoped for, the evidence of things not seen.*

*Hebrews 11:1*

If we were to research the definition of the word faith, we would find that it is defined as the firm belief in something in which there is no proof. In other words, faith is believing in what appears to be impossible. Our focus scripture is one that we have heard over and over throughout not only our walk with Christ, but through the trying journeys that we have to endure. It is in this scripture that we become aware that faith is what allows us to hope in what we cannot see. It gives us sight that we did not know we had. The more you have to rely on faith, the more you will begin to realize that there are different kinds of faith. We will discuss unprecedented faith and "now faith."

Unprecedented faith is the prerequisite to now faith. Depending on where you are and what you are believing God for, you may have to be willing to put your pride to the side and walk in a way that does not appear normal to people. Be okay with this, because although your process may not seem normal in the eyes of others, the blessing that you obtain in the end will be the very thing that blesses the ones who could not understand your posture throughout your process.

Unprecedented faith is faith that has never been done or known before. This is a new level of faith that will surprise even you. It is unparalleled, out of the ordinary, unusual, and unique. Unprecedented faith is the faith that will cause others to look at you and question your sanity. They will look and listen to your beliefs and come to the conclusion that you are crazy but in reality, you are in a place where you just believe God for the impossible. This unprecedented faith will suddenly give you courage when you feel as if you're at the end of your rope. Unprecedented faith reveals to us who we truly are. We learn our strengths and how to overcome our weaknesses. If you have unusual faith, then you can count on an unusual blessing coming to you. Your measure of faith determines the measure of your blessing.

Before long, we will come to the realization that "now faith" is what you do. It is how you react at the very moment you find yourself at wits end. It is "now faith" that brings you to a place where you can make it through when nothing around you seems to make sense. The harder things gets, the more you will realize faith is the key to pull you through.

As life moves forward, and you experience different things, your level of faith should increase and grow stronger over time. The level of faith you needed to conqueror you last season cannot be enough to help you overcome where you currently are. Ever heard the saying, "New levels, new devils"? Well because each new level you embark upon has its own share of trials, that same level will need its own measure of faith if you plan to make it through. It is "now faith" that helps you determine in your mind that regardless of what you may be facing, you have what it takes to conqueror it all. Truth be told, without faith, most of us would be dead by now.

Hebrews 11:6 tells us that without faith, it is impossible to please God. Can you imagine the heaviness that would come with knowing that everything you've done never impressed God because you lacked the faith to believe that he could bring about the very thing that you expected? We have to please God even when we are being tried. It becomes so challenging because there are times when God intentionally allows us to be tried. So how do we intentionally strive to please someone who has put us in a predicament where we are hurt, torn, and do not know how we will make it to the end? This is when it becomes necessary to put faith before feelings.

Every person should know that feelings and emotions can lead you down a path of destruction because they are so shallow. Sometimes our feelings have no depth and lead us nowhere. This is why it is necessary for our faith to overtake our feelings. When we step out of what we feel and tap into what we believe, things will begin to change. Faith and feelings cannot reside in the same place. How many times have you heard, "Either you will believe or you won't"? This holds true here. When it comes to activating faith, we cannot be wishy washy. We must make a decision, take a stand and declare that regardless of what we feel, we will not allow our feelings to take the place of our faith.

Faith is supposed to be that thing that carries us to the other side, but sometimes it seems that it is the very thing that is keeping us stuck where we are. You believed that with faith you would obtain, but it didn't happen when you wanted it to. I find that one of our biggest issues is that we throw temper tantrums when God does not move in ways that we expect him to move. How dare we expect God to operate in the box we set before him. God does not operate under the circumstances that we consider to be normal. So holding God to our expectations gives him no room to do exceeding abundantly above all we could ask or think (Ephesians 3:20). So God not doing as we would desire is not denial, it is him preparing to give us more than we could have asked for.

Faith can sometimes be the hardest thing to stand on. You had faith that God would bring you out, but you found yourself still in the fire. You had faith that something out there was better than this, but you didn't know how to get it. What do you do when it seems as if your faith has betrayed you? What do you do when it seems as if your faith has failed? The one thing that was supposed to help you seems to be hurting you. What do you do when faith seems to be your worst enemy? What do you do when the relevant factor that should influence your come-up seems to be embarrassing you?

Everyone will not be able to comprehend your faith, because everyone is not enduring your storm. Your faith is an agreement between you and God, concerning where you go next. That is an intimate connection that should not be influenced by the voices and opinions of others. What we must realize is that the race we are running is sure. God has already destined for us to be victorious. We cannot give up because things seem to be overtaking us but rather, we should stand tall and stand firm on our faith because we are close to the finish line.

As the days progress in your storm, that brings you closer to the end. If we would divert our thinking to being closer to the end instead of another day in turmoil, we would see that the storm doesn't last that long. How are you spending your days in the wait? Are you constantly looking at where you are or are you allowing your faith to prepare you for where you are going? Faith gives us the energy to withstand what we have to endure.

# Key Points

# Key Points

# After the Battle

*But the God of all grace, who hath called us unto his eternal glory by Christ Jesus, after that ye have suffered a while, make you perfect, stablish, strengthen, settle you.*

*1 Peter 5:10*

After the battle is a very celebratory time. For so long, you have been expecting to win and finally, your victory is tangible. As exciting of a time as this may be, it is important that we do not forget to tell God "thank you." God has brought us through a lot and he has equally given us just as much. We should not become so consumed with our blessing that we forget to acknowledge the blessor. Not only should you thank him at the time when he gives you what you have been fighting for, but you should thank him often. After all, you prayed often while you were fighting. Execute that same energy even after you have received the blessing. Be consistent in thanksgiving. Consistence in thanksgiving shows God that even after a blessing, he can count on you to still be faithful to him.

Be sure to take care of your blessing once you receive it. How unfortunate would it be to lose what you have prayed for because you mishandled and mistreated it? Don't become so comfortable with your blessing that you allow it to lose its significance to you. If it was important before, it should be even more important now that it's in your hands.

As much as we may think that our battle is one of a kind, most likely, someone somewhere is going through the same thing. God did not bring you out of your storm for you to keep your testimony a secret. Share your testimony because it could be the very thing that someone else needs to make it through their own trials. Your strength and courage could encourage someone so much that they decide to continue on instead of giving up. While you may have been blessed in the end, your battle had a deeper meaning that is usually not discovered until later. Are you willing to acknowledge the deeper meaning when it reveals itself?

Consider how your blessing has come at the right time. Although the fight may have been treacherous, it prepared you for victory and it prepared you to keep the blessing once you received it. It is usually not until we receive what we have been hoping for that we realize it was placed in our hands at the right time. We begin to examine where we have been and admit that if we received this blessing any sooner, we would've destroyed it. But that's the thing about God's timing—even when we feel like we need something now, God allows us to wait because his timing is perfect.

It is crucial that we remain humble after our fight, being careful not to boast but to live in true gratefulness. God is excited that he has been able to release something that has been anticipated for so long, and it is up to us to remain in a humble state of mind so that we can keep what we now have. The Lord gives and he takes away (Job 1:21). None of us wants to lose what we've worked so hard for. So as you continue on your journey of victory, remember the blessor, take care of the blessing, share your testimony, and never take for granted what God has done in your life.

# Key Points

# Key Points

# About the Author

Natai Billops is an ambitious and driven young woman. She has a positive outlook on life and lives life to its fullest. Having credentials from Delaware State University and recently receiving a Master's degree from Temple University, she seeks out opportunities and challenges that will strengthen her ability to grow and develop into a more successful young person.

Natai has a passion to inspire and empower all people, young and old, to reach their highest potential; this is reflected in her first book release *Positive Vibez*. Launching the "Positive Vibez" tshirt line, she has devoted her time to several different areas to encourage, strengthen, and help others.

Witnessing the struggles that come with the beginning stages of entrepreneurship, Natai initiated Young, Saved, & Paid, which is geared toward helping Christian entrepreneurs with business startup and management.

She did not stop there. Being a proud member of Alpha Kappa Alpha Sorority, Inc., Natai realized there was no safe haven for Christians in the Divine Nine organizations. So she took the initiative and developed Saved & Greek, a community made especially for Christian Greeks. This community allows Christian Greeks to freely express their love for God as well as their respective organizations.

As a gifted communicator, she is straightforward, open-minded, and truthful in both her speaking and in her writing. She takes pride in her personal relationship with God and seeks his face for clear direction and instructions. It is her hope that everyone she encounters will be moved to be better people.

www.ingramcontent.com/pod-product-compliance
Lightning Source LLC
Chambersburg PA
CBHW071134090426
42736CB00012B/2121